mrjc
8/11

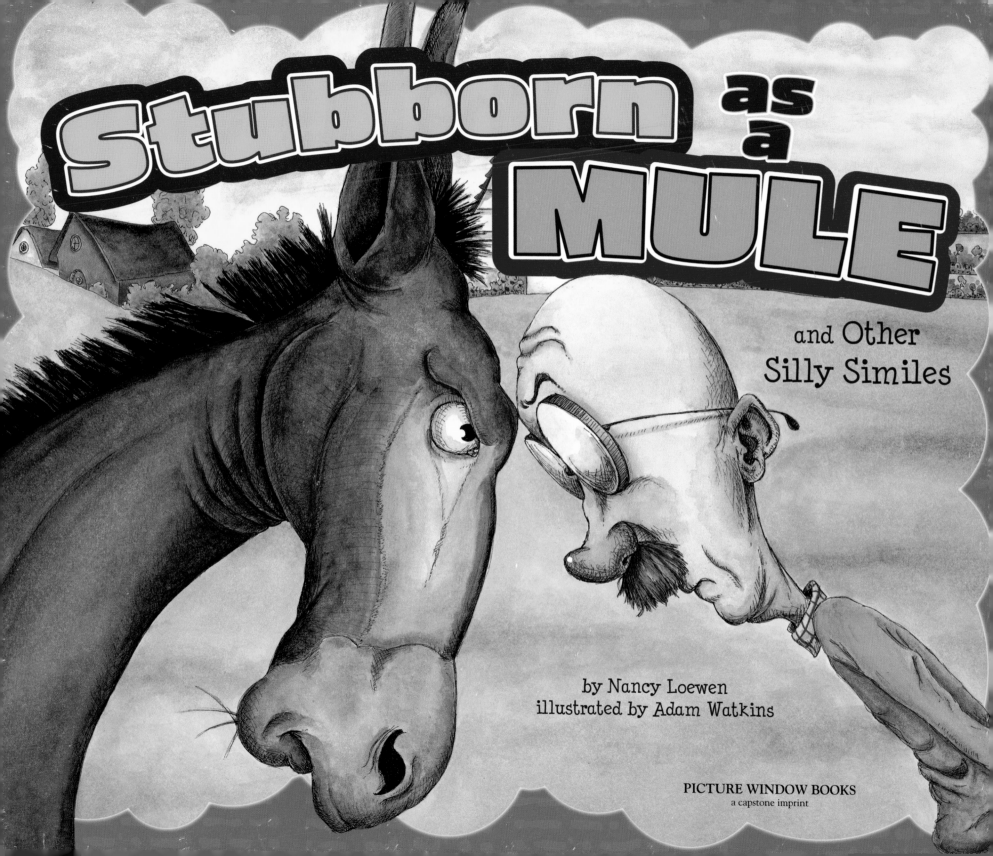

Stubborn as a MULE

and Other Silly Similes

by Nancy Loewen
illustrated by Adam Watkins

PICTURE WINDOW BOOKS
a capstone imprint

What is a simile?

To Mia and her Papa—A.W.

Editor: Jill Kalz
Designer: Lori Bye
Art Director: Nathan Gassman
Production Specialist: Sarah Bennett
The illustrations in this book were created with water color, pen, and ink.

Picture Window Books
151 Good Counsel Drive
P.O. Box 669
Mankato, MN 56002-0669
877-845-8392
www.capstonepub.com

 All books published by Picture Window Books are manufactured
with paper containing at least 10 percent post-consumer waste.

Library of Congress Cataloging-in-Publication Data
Loewen, Nancy, 1964-
   Stubborn as a mule and other silly similes / by Nancy Loewen ;
illustrated by Adam Watkins.
      p. cm. – (Ways to say it)
   Includes index.
   ISBN 978-1-4048-6271-5 (library binding)
   ISBN 978-1-4048-6715-4 (paperback)
   1. Simile–Juvenile literature. I. Watkins, Adam, ill. II. Title.
   PE1445.S5L64 2011
   428.1–dc22   2010033763

Special thanks to our adviser, Terry Flaherty, PhD,
Professor of English, Minnesota State University, Mankato,
for his expertise.

Printed in the United States of America in North Mankato, Minnesota.
092010   005933CGS11

Similes can be **as easy as pie**

or **as hard as nails.**

They might **cry like babies**

or **chatter like monkeys.**

A simile is a figure of speech that compares two things. These things are different in most ways. But they're alike in at least one way. A simile shows us what the two things have in common. Similes usually use the connecting words "like" or "as." Turn the page to meet Mr. Moe, and see how similes can make a story more colorful.

Meet Mr. Moe.

Here, Mr. Moe's head and an egg are being compared. Both are round and smooth. "As bald as an egg" is a simile.

Metaphors can be used to compare things too. Metaphors don't use "like" or "as." If we said, "Mr. Moe's head is an egg," we would be using a metaphor.

Mr. Moe is **AS BALD AS AN EGG.**

He doesn't have any hair. At all. Not even one!

Mr. Moe is **as tall as a giraffe ...** ...and **as thin as a rail.**

Mark Twain used the phrase "as thin as a rail" in his book *Roughing It*, published in 1872. He was describing a skinny, sickly woman: "You'll marry a combination of calico and consumption that's as thin as a rail."

Today Mr. Moe is going out. He's meeting someone very special for lunch. He wants to look GOOD.

He polishes his shoes until they

shine like a new penny.

SH OLISH KIT

8

He puts on
his best hat.

It **FITS LIKE A GLOVE.**

Similes often appeal to our senses. A new penny gleams. It catches our eye. And when we think about slipping our hands into a pair of gloves, we understand that Mr. Moe's hat fits him well.

Mr. Moe hurries down the street.

Oh, no! A gust of wind blows off his hat.

10

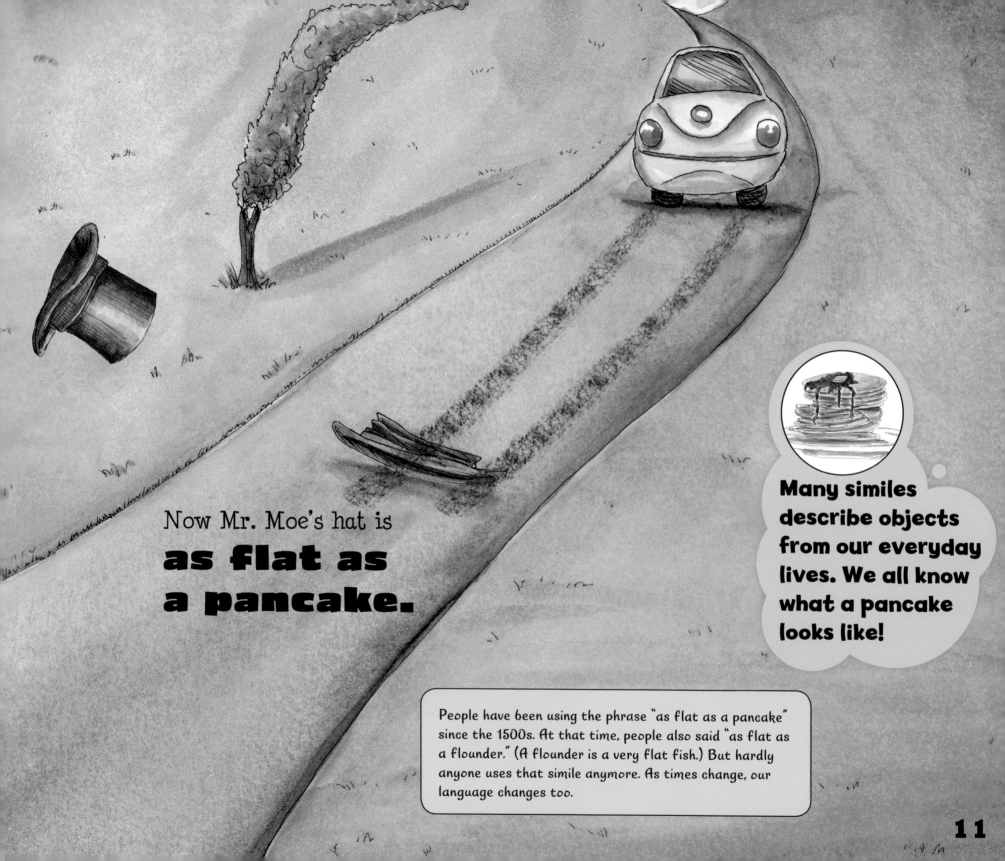

Now Mr. Moe's hat is
as flat as a pancake.

Many similes describe objects from our everyday lives. We all know what a pancake looks like!

People have been using the phrase "as flat as a pancake" since the 1500s. At that time, people also said "as flat as a flounder." (A flounder is a very flat fish.) But hardly anyone uses that simile anymore. As times change, our language changes too.

At the store, a lady tries to snatch the last tin of taffy from Mr. Moe's hands.

Mr. Moe really wants that taffy. He holds on tight.

But the lady is **as stubborn as a mule.**

Similes can be used to describe a person's actions and feelings. This simile isn't saying the lady *looks* like a mule. It's saying she's *behaving* like a mule. She wants to do things her way.

Mr. Moe leaves empty-handed.

The simile "as stubborn as a mule" has been in use since the 1800s. At that time, mules were work animals—they did the tasks that trucks and tractors do today. When mules don't want to work, they are nearly impossible to budge!

Mr. Moe decides to buy flowers instead.

He taps his foot.

The line moves

at a snail's pace.

Sometimes, similes don't use connecting words, but they still compare two things. Here, the phrase "at a snail's pace" means that the line is moving slowly. You could also say the line is moving "like a snail" or "as slow as a snail."

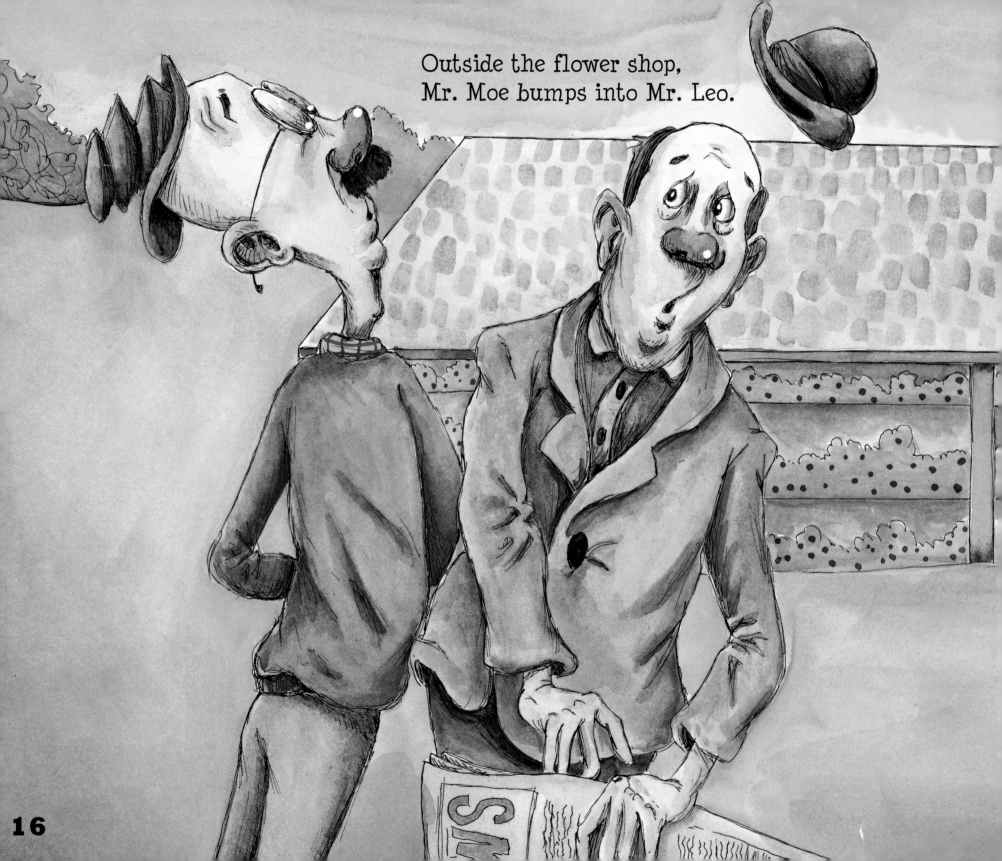

Outside the flower shop,
Mr. Moe bumps into Mr. Leo.

16

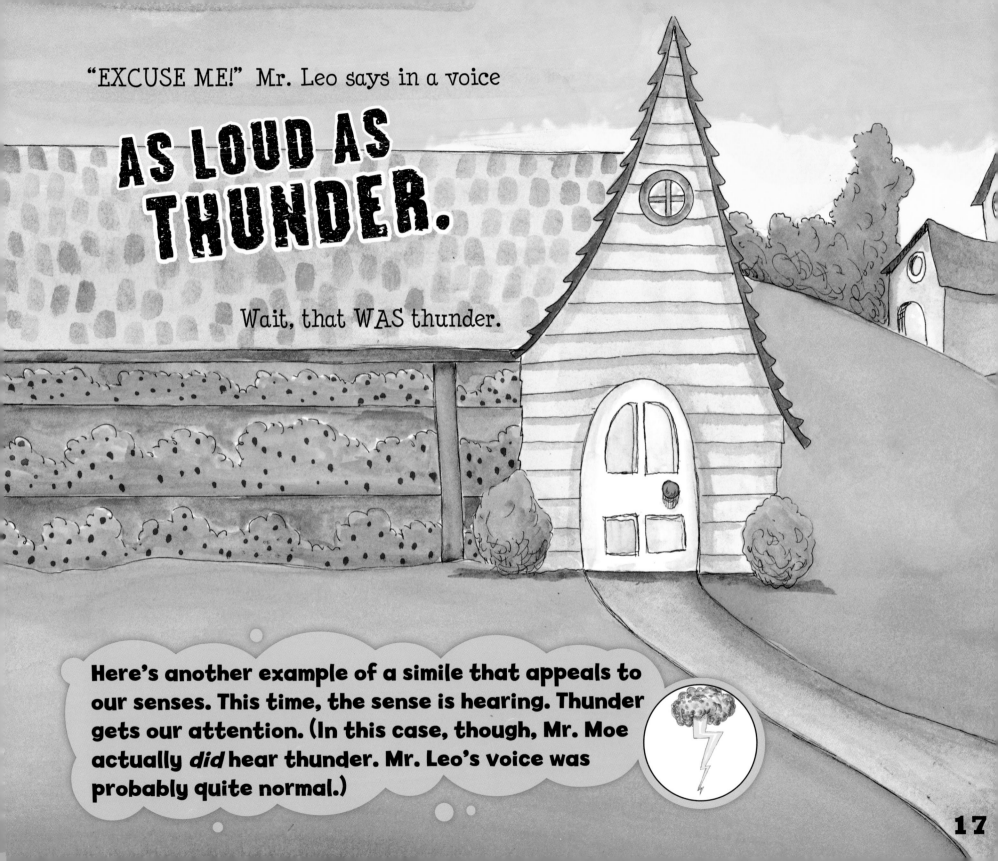

"EXCUSE ME!" Mr. Leo says in a voice

AS LOUD AS THUNDER.

Wait, that WAS thunder.

Here's another example of a simile that appeals to our senses. This time, the sense is hearing. Thunder gets our attention. (In this case, though, Mr. Moe actually *did* hear thunder. Mr. Leo's voice was probably quite normal.)

A few raindrops fall ... and a few more ... and now Mr. Moe is standing in a downpour.

He's

as wet as a fish.

And if he doesn't hurry, he'll be late!

Similes often include descriptive words that make the comparison more clear. "Wet" is a descriptive word. If we just said Mr. Moe was "like a fish," we wouldn't know *how* he's like a fish. Is he scaly? Smelly? The word "wet" lets us know that Mr. Moe is as wet as if he were living in water, the way a fish does.

The café is crowded.

Mr. Moe wishes he had eyes **LIKE A HAWK**. Where is his special someone?

Then Mr. Moe hears a voice that's **like music to his ears.**

"OVER HERE, GRANDPA!"

Similes can sum up complex ideas in just a few words. Hawks have excellent eyesight. They can spot something small, like a mouse, from a great distance. Mr. Moe sees lots of people in the café, but he wants to find one certain person.

Mr. Moe's hat is ruined. He didn't get his taffy. He's soaked to the skin.

But sitting beside his granddaughter, he's

as happy as a lark.

A lark is a kind of songbird. Picture it perched on a branch, singing. Doesn't that make you feel cheerful? That's how Mr. Moe is feeling when he finally sees his granddaughter!

Filling the Blanks Like a _____

The similes in this book are ones that are commonly used. But there's no reason you can't make up your own.

Look at these well-known similes:
as quiet as a mouse
runs like a deer
as sweet as honey
sings like a bird

Now take off the last word, and brainstorm for words to replace it. You can add more than one word if you want. For example, "as quiet as a mouse" could become "as quiet as a <u>sleeping kitten</u>."

Next, try taking off the first word (not including "as"). You could say "as <u>tiny</u> as a mouse" or "as <u>sneaky</u> as a mouse," for example.

Are you up for a challenge? Try this one!

As nervous as a long-tailed cat in a roomful of rocking chairs.

As _____ as a _____ in a _____ of _____.

To Learn More

More Books to Read

Cleary, Brian. *Skin Like Milk, Hair of Silk: What Are Similes and Metaphors?* Words Are CATegorical. Minneapolis: Millbrook Press, 2009.

Fandel, Jennifer. *Metaphors, Similes, and Other Word Pictures.* Understanding Poetry. Mankato, Minn.: Creative Education, 2004.

Leedy, Loreen. *Crazy Like a Fox: A Simile Story.* New York: Holiday House, 2008.

Internet Sites

FactHound offers a safe, fun way to find Internet sites related to this book. All of the sites on FactHound have been researched by our staff.

Here's all you do:
Visit *www.facthound.com*
Type in this code: 9781404862715

Check out projects, games and lots more at **www.capstonekids.com**

Glossary

compare—to look closely at things to discover ways they are alike or different

complex—having many parts

descriptive—making a picture with words

exaggerate—to overstate something; for example, to describe something as being bigger or smaller than it actually is

figure of speech—a word or words that create an effect without using their real meaning; a simile is a figure of speech

metaphor—a figure of speech that compares different things without using "like" or "as"

phrase—a group of words that are used together

simile—a figure of speech that compares different things using "like" or "as"

Index

Look for all the books in the Ways to Say It series:

She Sells Seashells and Other Tricky Tongue Twisters
Stubborn as a Mule and Other Silly Similes
Talking Turkey and Other Clichés We Say
You're Toast and Other Metaphors We Adore